PLEASING THE FATHER

GLORIA COPELAND

KENNETH COPELAND PUBLICATIONS
FORT WORTH, TEXAS

Pleasing the Father

ISBN 1-57562-121-5   30-0543

© 1996 Kenneth Copeland Publications

All scripture is from the *King James Version* unless otherwise noted.

Kenneth Copeland Publications
Fort Worth, Texas 76192-0001

Pleasing the Father

Right now I'm hungrier for God than I have ever been in my life. I'm hungry to know Him better. I'm hungry for a greater manifestation of His presence. I'm hungry for Jesus to be fully formed in me.

I'm not alone in that desire. Far from it. Everywhere I go, I see believers who are desiring more of God. I meet Christians whose hearts are crying out to be changed and filled with greater degrees of the glory of God.

A sense of urgency has been implanted in our spirit by the Spirit of God because the end of this age is very near. Time is running out, and God is fulfilling His plan in us. He is preparing for Himself a glorious Church without spot or wrinkle. He is raising up a people who will walk in the things He has prepared for them.

God is bringing forth a multitude of believers who will fulfill the divine destiny prepared for them since the beginning of time. That destiny is defined clearly in Romans 8:29:

> **For those whom [God] foreknew— of whom He was aware and loved beforehand—He also destined from the beginning (foreordaining them) to be molded into the image of His Son [and share inwardly His like- ness], that He might become the first-born among many brethren *(The Amplified Bible).***

Our destiny as believers is to grow up in Jesus. It's to be fully conformed to His image which was placed within us the moment we were born again.

It's a staggering thought that you and I could ever truly be transformed into that divine image. It seems almost impossible that we could be like Jesus. But God says we can be. In fact, the Bible says He has equipped us with everything necessary so that we might continue growing and developing:

> **Until we all attain oneness in the faith and in the comprehension of the full and accurate knowledge of the Son of God; that [we might arrive] at really mature manhood— the completeness of personality which is nothing less than the standard height of Christ's own perfection—the measure of the stature of the fullness of the Christ, and the completeness found in Him (Ephesians 4:13, *The Amplified Bible*).**

If anyone other than the Spirit of God had written that, I wouldn't be able to believe it. But the Spirit of God *did* write it! So as amazing as it seems, we must simply believe that He has the ability to conform us to Jesus so completely that we *"...become a body wholly filled and flooded with God Himself!"* (Ephesians 3:19, *The Amplified Bible*).

We Must Do Our Part

Not only is God able to do that, it is His will for us. It is His end-time plan. But whether or not that divine will comes to pass in our own individual lives is up to us. If we want to *be a part* of God's plan, we must *do our part* of God's plan.

That's how it has always been. In Genesis 18:19, God said of Abraham: *"For I know him, that he will command his children and his household after him, and they shall keep the way of the Lord, to do justice and judgment; that the Lord may bring upon Abraham that which he hath spoken of him."*

Abraham's part was to cooperate with the Lord. If Abraham didn't do that, if he didn't obey what God told him to do, God couldn't fulfill His promise to make Abraham a father of many nations, even though it was God's will.

The same is true for us today. It is God's will that we be conformed to the image of Jesus. It is His will to manifest Himself in our lives just as He manifested Himself through Jesus' life. But He cannot do it until we do our part.

Our part is simply this: *to walk pleasing before Him—to think His thoughts, to speak His words. In other words, to walk in His ways.*

If we want to fulfill our divine destiny and enjoy the fullness of the power of God in our lives, we must make a decision and a determination to stop living to please ourselves and start living every moment of every day to please the Father. We must walk out the prayer the Apostle Paul prayed for the Colossians:

...That ye might be filled with the knowledge of [God's] will in all wisdom and spiritual understanding; That ye might walk worthy of the Lord unto all pleasing, being fruitful in every good work, and increasing in the knowledge of God; Strengthened with all might, according to his glorious power... (Colossians 1:9-11).

Notice that verse connects pleasing the Lord with the manifestation of God's glorious power. It says they come together.

The life of Jesus was proof. He said, *"He that sent me is with me: the Father hath not left me alone; for I do always those things that please him"* (John 8:29).

We talk a lot about the fact that God will never leave us nor forsake us. And it's true, He is always with us. But we have to admit, His power is not always in manifestation.

In Jesus' life, however, God's power was constantly in manifestation. Every moment of every hour of every day, Jesus walked in the measureless, manifested power and presence of God because He always did those things that pleased the Father.

I am able to do nothing from Myself—independently, of My own accord—but as I am taught by God and as I get His orders. [I decide as I am bidden to decide. As the voice comes to Me, so I give a decision.] Even as I hear, I judge and My judgment is right (just, righteous), because I do not seek or consult My own will—I have no desire to do what is pleasing to Myself, My own aim, My own purpose—but only the will and pleasure of the Father Who sent Me (John 5:30, _The Amplified Bible_).

And He Who sent Me is ever with Me; My Father has not left Me alone, for I always do what pleases Him (John 8:29, *The Amplified Bible*).

God was able to say of Him, *"Thou art my beloved Son, in whom I am well pleased"* (Mark 1:11).

Light...Not Twilight!

There's no reason why we as believers can't please God as much as Jesus did. We have a reborn spirit made in His image. We've been given His righteousness. We've been filled with the same Holy Spirit. We have all the capacity that Jesus had in the earth to be just like Him and to do the works that He did because He lives in us. The scripture says *"...Christ in you, the hope of glory"* (Colossians 1:27).

He was dedicated. He was totally sold out to God. He was without sin. The Bible tells us many times He ministered to the multitudes all day and then prayed all night, yet Jesus had a flesh and blood body just like yours and mine. He enjoyed a good night's sleep just as much as we do. So there was an element of crucifying the flesh involved in giving up that sleep and doing what pleased God. He had to say *no* to His flesh, and *yes* to the Father.

"Well, Gloria, I know Jesus did that, but God doesn't expect that kind of self-sacrifice from us."

Yes, He does. First Peter 4:1-3 says:

So, since Christ suffered in the flesh [for us, for you], arm yourselves with the same thought and purpose [patiently to suffer rather than fail to please God]. For whoever has suffered in the flesh [having the mind of Christ] has done with [intentional] sin—has stopped pleasing himself and the world, and pleases God. So that he can no longer spend the rest of his natural life living by [his] human appetites and desires, but

[he lives] for what God wills. For the time that is past already suffices for doing what the Gentiles like to do... *(The Amplified Bible).*

It's time for the Church to stop living like gentiles (or the sinners) do! It's time for the Church to live like God says, regardless of what the world around us is doing. Just because the morals of the world slip doesn't mean the morals in the Church should slip.

It doesn't matter how dark this world becomes, we are to be the light of this world. Not the *twilight* of the world—the *light!*

We need to fight against compromise by arming ourselves with the commitment to suffer in the flesh rather than fail to please God. To suffer in the flesh doesn't mean to bear sickness and poverty without complaining. Jesus already bore sickness and poverty for us along with every other curse of the law so that we can be free from those things. We are expected to resist that curse in Jesus' Name.

Suffering in the flesh is making your flesh do something it doesn't want to do. It's dedicating yourself to do what's pleasing to God even when it causes your flesh discomfort.

When you're ready to do that, you'll go beyond just "not sinning" and into a life that's pleasing to God. You'll be ready to lay down those things that you enjoy, things that aren't necessarily bad in themselves, yet they are hindering your walk with God.

If you want to walk in the best God has for you, those are the kinds of sacrifices you must make, for Jesus said:

He who does not take up his cross and follow Me [that is, cleave steadfastly to Me, conforming

wholly to My example in living and if need be in dying also] is not worthy of Me. Whoever finds his [lower] life will lose [the higher life], and whosoever loses his [lower] life on My account will find [the higher life] (Matthew 10:38-39, *The Amplified Bible*).

If you could see what God has for you in the higher life, you would immediately let go of the mundane things of the world. You would drop that junk so fast you wouldn't even know which way it went. But you're not going to be able to see it and then make your decision.

You have to step into that higher life by faith. You have to lay down your life because the Word says to do it. Then and only then will you discover the wonders that are waiting on the other side of your obedience.

I'm sure Enoch didn't know what the higher life held for him. He probably had no idea that he'd be the first man ever raptured. But he was. Hebrews 11:5 says, *"By faith Enoch was translated that he should not see death...for before his translation he had this testimony, that* he pleased God."

Righteousness and Holiness: Two Different Things

How do you develop the spiritual strength to do the things that please the Father rather than the things that please yourself? First and foremost by spending time in the Word and in prayer. When the power of God was being displayed through the early apostles in great signs and wonders, that's what they were doing. They were giving themselves *"continually to prayer, and to the ministry of the word"* (Acts 6:4).

Romans 8 says it this way: *"For they that are after the flesh do mind the things of the flesh; but they that are after the Spirit the things of the Spirit"* (verse 5).

That is the matter in a nutshell. If you want to grow physically and build big muscles, you have to spend time lifting weights and doing physical things to build those muscles. If you want to grow spiritually, you will have to spend time doing spiritual things.

As you spend time fellowshiping with God in His Word, by the power of that Word the Holy Spirit will separate you not only from sin, but also from the unnecessary things of life. He will impart to you the spiritual might and grace you need to obey the instructions in Ephesians 4:22-24:

Strip yourselves of your former nature—put off and discard your old unrenewed self—which characterized your previous manner of life and becomes corrupt through lusts and desires that spring from delusion; And be constantly renewed in the spirit of your mind—having a fresh mental and spiritual attitude; And put on the new nature

(the regenerate self) created in God's image, (Godlike) in true righteousness and holiness *(The Amplified Bible).*

That verse tells us that righteousness and holiness are two different things. Righteousness is the right-standing with God you gained when you were born again. The only thing you did to be made righteous was to make Jesus Christ the Lord of your life.

Holiness, however, is another matter. You are not *made* holy. Holiness is the result of your choices. It's what you do with your time and your actions. It's your conduct. It comes when you make a decision of your will to live according to the precepts of the Lord. In short, holiness is doing those things that please the Father.

To be holy is to be *"sanctified, and meet for the master's use"* (2 Timothy 2:21). Sanctified means *set apart*. Set apart from what? From the world! God wants us to be so caught up in spiritual things that we lose interest in carnal activities and pursue Him with all our hearts.

He doesn't want us simply to obey a set of rules because it's the "right thing to do." That's law instead of spirit. God wants us to live holy lives because we have a heartfelt desire to please Him. When we spend time with the Lord, we *want* to do the things that please Him. Our desire is for spiritual things, not the things of the flesh. It shouldn't be a "head thing" but a "heart thing." Time with Him separates us to Him. He wants us to love Him so much that we want to be wholly dedicated to Him!

And He doesn't want us to consider such holiness as something out of the ordinary. He wants us to take the attitude of the Apostle Paul who said to the believers at Rome:

I beseech you therefore, brethren, by the mercies of God, that ye present

your bodies a living sacrifice, holy, acceptable unto God, which is your reasonable service. And be not conformed to this world: but be ye transformed by the renewing of your mind, that ye may prove what is that good, and acceptable, and perfect, will of God (Romans 12:1-2).

Being wholly dedicated to God is your reasonable service. It's not something above and beyond the call of duty. It's not something that is just expected of preachers and ministers. God expects us all to live holy. He says, *"Be ye holy; for I am holy"* (1 Peter 1:16).

Certainly such a life will require us to make some sacrifices. It will cause us to suffer in the flesh at times. But it will be worth it. For *"the sufferings of this present time are not worthy to be compared with the glory which shall be revealed in us"* (Romans 8:18).

When you see the power and glory of God start to flow in greater measure through you, you won't regret you made those sacrifices; you'll be glad! When you lay hands on a crippled person and see him raised instantly out of a wheelchair, you'll be glad you turned down that carnal movie your friends went to see. You'll be glad that you gave up those hours of sleep so you could spend extra time in the Word and in prayer.

When you speak in the Name of Jesus to someone in bondage, and the devil instantly flees and they go free, you won't be wishing you'd spent more time pleasing yourself, you'll be thanking God you chose to please Him instead.

You may think I'm being overly dramatic, but I'm not. Those things are going to happen—not just at the hands of famous preachers and full-time ministers, but at the hands of everyday believers. We've already started to see it. But we're just on the edge of what's coming. We haven't seen anything yet!

The prophets of God are telling us that we are about to see the greatest outpouring of God's power this earth has ever known. It's been said that if we were told all that's about to happen, we would not be able to believe it because the magnitude of it is so great.

Glory to God, we are about to see multitudes of Christians put aside the distractions of this age and rise up in the strength of God Himself! We are about to see believers conformed to the image of Jesus! We are about to see the Church God has always dreamed of—a Church holy and without blemish!

Determine in your heart to be a part of it all. Make up your mind that you won't be sidelined by doing petty things that please yourself. Dedicate yourself to live wholly pleasing to the Father and get ready for a life of power!

Prayer for Salvation and Baptism in the Holy Spirit

Heavenly Father, I come to You in the Name of Jesus. Your Word says, *"...whosoever shall call on the name of the Lord shall be saved"* (Acts 2:21). I am calling on You. I pray and ask Jesus to come into my heart and be Lord over my life according to Romans 10:9-10. *"If thou shalt confess with thy mouth the Lord Jesus, and shalt believe in thine heart that God hath raised him from the dead, thou shalt be saved."* I do that now. I confess that Jesus is Lord, and I believe in my heart that God raised Him from the dead.

I am now reborn! I am a Christian—a child of Almighty God! I am saved! You also said in Your Word, *"If ye then, being evil, know how to give good gifts unto your children: HOW MUCH MORE shall your heavenly Father give the Holy Spirit to them that ask him?"* (Luke 11:13). I'm also asking You to fill me with the Holy Spirit. Holy Spirit, rise up within me as I praise God. I fully expect to speak with other tongues as You give me the utterance (Acts 2:4).

Begin to praise God for filling you with the Holy Spirit. Speak those words and syllables you receive—not in your own language, but the language given to you by the Holy Spirit. You have to use your own voice. God will not force you to speak.

Now you are a Spirit-filled believer. Continue with the blessing God has given you and pray in tongues each day. You'll never be the same!

Find a good Word of God preaching church, and become a part of a church family who will love and care for you as you love and care for them.

We need to be hooked up to each other. It increases our strength in God. It's God's plan for us.

Books by Kenneth Copeland

Books by Gloria Copeland

*   And Jesus Healed Them All
Are You Ready?
Build Yourself an Ark
From Faith to Faith—A Daily Guide to Victory
God's Prescription for Divine Health
God's Success Formula
God's Will for You
God's Will for Your Healing
God's Will Is Prosperity
God's Will Is the Holy Spirit
*   Harvest of Health
Healing Promises
Love—The Secret to Your Success
No Deposit—No Return
Pressing In—It's Worth It All
The Power to Live a New Life
The Unbeatable Spirit of Faith
*   Walk in the Spirit
Walk With God
Well Worth the Wait

*   Available in Spanish

Other Books Published by KCP

*   Heirs Together by Mac Hammond
John G. Lake—His Life, His Sermons,
    His Boldness of Faith
Winning the World by Mac Hammond

World Offices
of Kenneth Copeland Ministries

For more information about KCM and a
free catalog, please write the office nearest you:

Kenneth Copeland Ministries
Fort Worth, Texas 76192-0001

Kenneth Copeland
Locked Bag 2600
Mansfield Delivery Centre
QUEENSLAND 4122
AUSTRALIA

Kenneth Copeland
Post Office Box 830
RANDBURG
2125
REPUBLIC OF SOUTH AFRICA

220123 MINSK
REPUBLIC OF BELARUS
Post Office 123
P/B 35
Kenneth Copeland Ministries

Kenneth Copeland
Post Office Box 15
BATH
BA1 1GD
ENGLAND

Kenneth Copeland
Post Office Box 58248
Vancouver
BRITISH COLUMBIA
V6P 6K1
CANADA